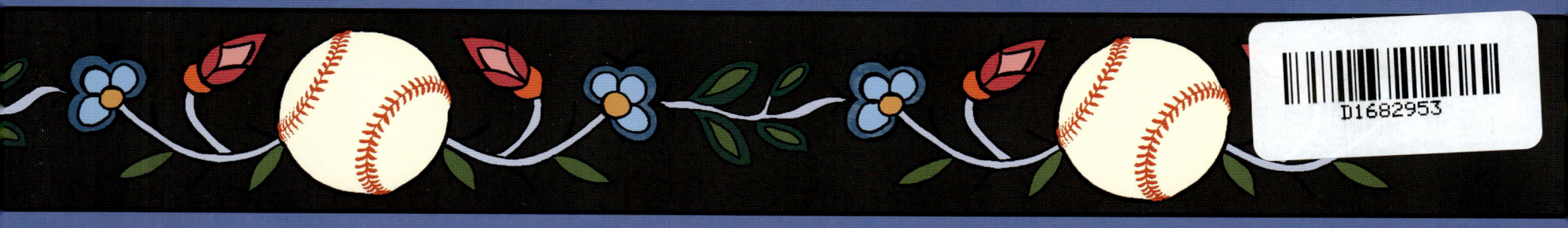

SHIBE PARK, PHILADELPHIA

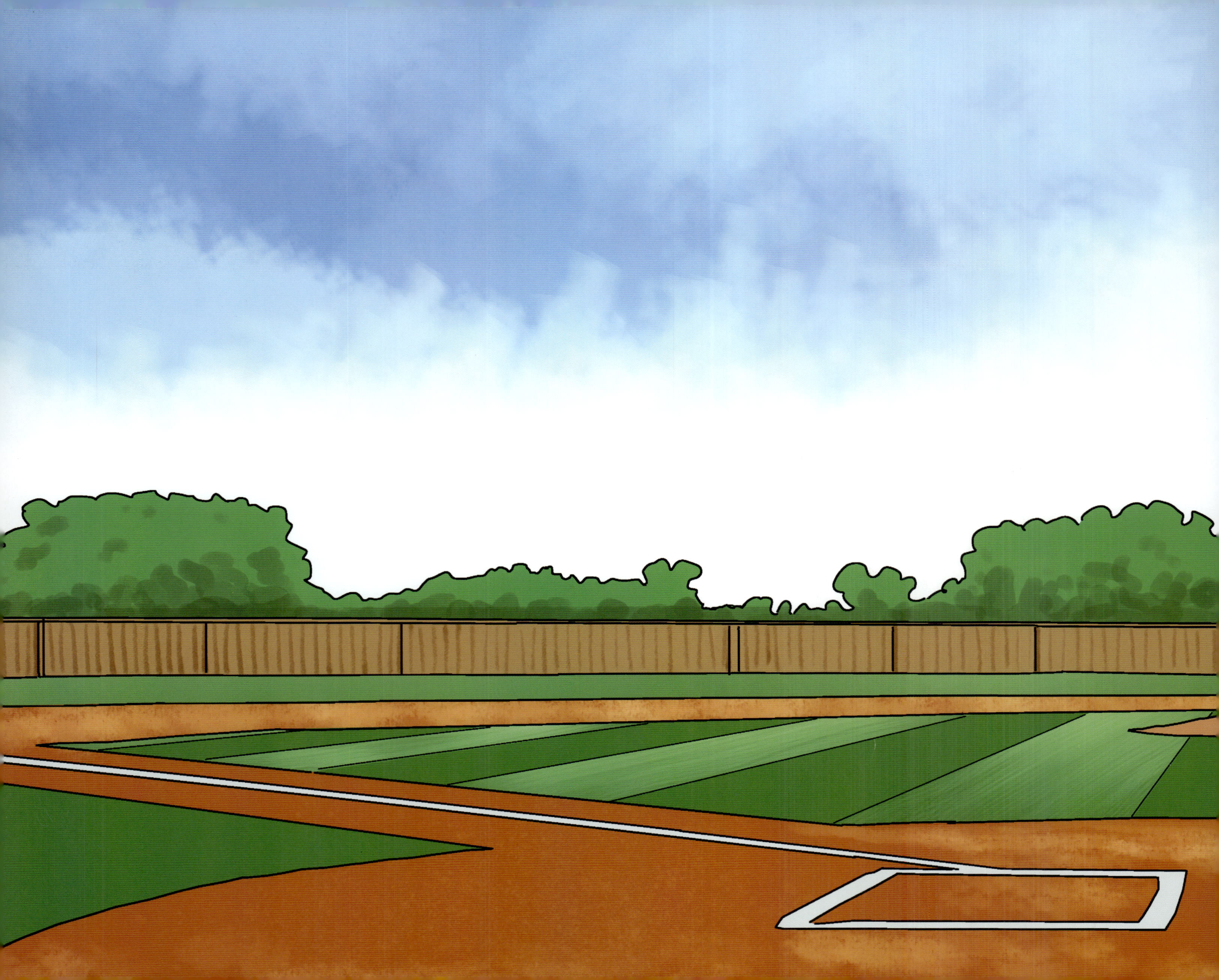

CONTENDERS
Two Native Baseball Players, One World Series

Written by **Traci Sorell** • Illustrated by **Arigon Starr**

BENDER

MEYERS

For Mark
—T. S.

Many thanks to the baseball fanatics in my life: my mother, Ruth; my sister, Gay; my father, Ken; and my grandparents, aunts, cousins, and dear friends who share my love of the game.
—A. S.

KOKILA
An imprint of Penguin Random House LLC, New York

First published in the United States of America by Kokila, an imprint of Penguin Random House LLC, 2023

Text copyright © 2023 by Traci Sorell
Illustrations copyright © 2023 by Arigon Starr

Penguin supports copyright. Copyright fuels creativity, encourages diverse voices, promotes free speech, and creates a vibrant culture. Thank you for buying an authorized edition of this book and for complying with copyright laws by not reproducing, scanning, or distributing any part of it in any form without permission. You are supporting writers and allowing Penguin to continue to publish books for every reader.

Kokila & colophon are registered trademarks of Penguin Random House LLC.

Visit us online at penguinrandomhouse.com.

Library of Congress Cataloging-in-Publication Data is available.

Manufactured in China

ISBN 9780593406472

1 3 5 7 9 10 8 6 4 2
TOPL

Design by Jasmin Rubero
Text set in Aleo

The publisher does not have any control over and does not assume any responsibility for author or third-party websites or their content.

―――

The art for this book was created with hand-drawn and digital elements, using archival photographs as reference. Lorene Sisquoc (Fort Sill Apache/Mountain Cahuilla) and Molly Murphy Adams (Oglala Lakota) were consulted and reviewed the Cahuilla and Ojibwe designs incorporated in the illustrations. Ms. Sisquoc is an expert basket weaver in addition to serving as the curator for the Sherman Indian Museum. Ms. Murphy Adams, a former Tulsa Artist Fellow, incorporates beadwork and printmaking into her contemporary artwork, which has become part of many permanent museum collections.

"Somebody has said that the only good Indian is a dead Indian,
but whoever he was, he never saw Bender and Meyers play ball."
—W. J. Lampton, *New York Times* reporter.

The insult Lampton quoted is credited to US Army General Philip Sheridan,
who is believed to have said it during a conversation with Comanche leader Tosahwi in 1869.

The World Waits

World Series.

1911.

Game One.

Bottom of the seventh inning.

Fifty telegraphers stand ready to share the action taking place in New York with Los Angeles, Havana, Tokyo, and around the globe.

John Meyers grips his bat.
Charles Bender stands tall on the mound.
Two friends making history. John and Charles are the first two citizens of Native Nations to play against each other in the baseball championship. With the score tied at one, Charles winds up.

Fires the pitch. And . . .

The Hit

THWACK! John doubles to left field.

The next batter smacks another double.

John speeds home from second—and scores! His winning run puts the New York Giants up one game to none against Charles's team, the Philadelphia Athletics.

Indian versus Indian

Newspapers recount the match as "Indian against Indian." They call Charles and John "Chief Bender" and "Chief Meyers" respectively—though neither is a tribal leader. The insults get worse. One reporter writes about the two "redskins," while another wonders, "Now who's the best Indian?"

John and Charles can't just show up and compete like their teammates. White fans, other players, managers, and sportswriters constantly hurl slights and slurs about their Native heritage. Charles and John are no strangers to challenges.

Charles's Childhood

Charles Albert Bender—"Al" to his family—grew up on the White Earth Reservation in northwestern Minnesota. His Ojibwe mother and German American father struggled to care for their large family.

At age seven, Al endured a long train ride with his two siblings and a few other Ojibwe children. The kids arrived at a year-round Indian boarding school in Philadelphia, Pennsylvania, funded in part by the federal Indian Department and run by the Episcopal Church. School life was strict, even abusive. Boys studied the Bible and performed manual labor like painting, installing windows, and farming.

For a time, Al worked in the school laundry room to help pay for his stay there. Summer breaks found the children sent to live with and work for white families in the country, harvesting crops and caring for animals on their farms. Al loved spending time in the woods and hunting when he got the chance.

Al also loved baseball. He learned the game by watching the older boys play. He even learned to make his own bats and balls like they did.

He thought he might be a catcher . . . until he got hit between the eyes with a pitch.

John's Childhood

John Tortes Meyers's family and friends had a nickname for him too: Jack. He learned to play baseball on his Cahuilla tribe's reservation in Southern California. Like Al, Jack had a German American father, but he died when Jack was seven. His Cahuilla mother, a skilled basket maker, worked as a hotel cook in nearby Riverside to support her children.

Despite the pressure during that time to adopt white people's norms, Jack spoke the Cahuilla language and stayed close to his family and culture.

He played baseball on the reservation and in Riverside and got his start by catching his older brother's pitches. Jack was curious and intelligent, although he wasn't able to finish school because he needed to work.

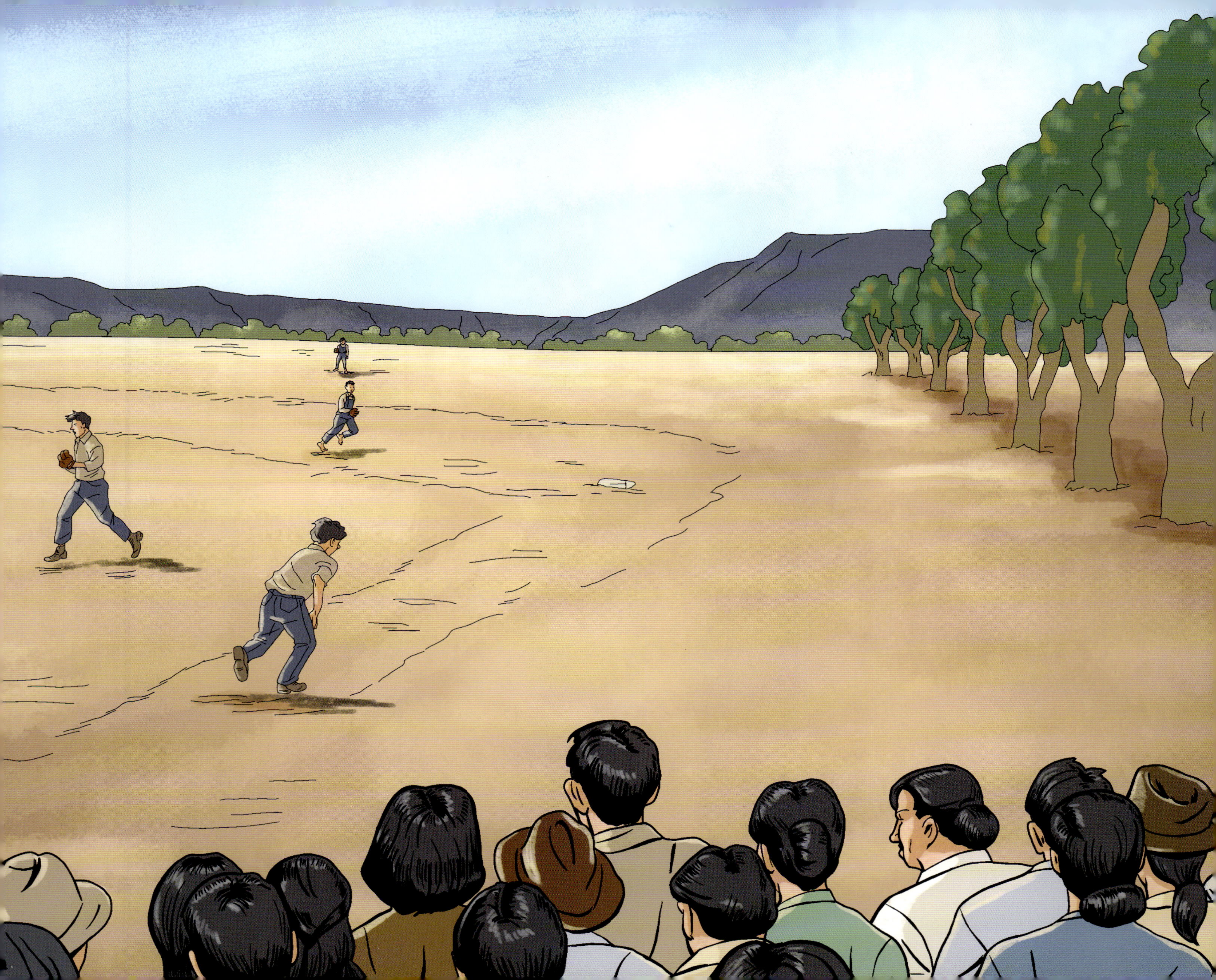

Charles's Teenage Years

Al finally returned to the White Earth Reservation from boarding school at age twelve. But life at home was still difficult and his father abusive. So Al and one of his older brothers ran away. That summer, they worked at another White Earth farm until a teacher from Carlisle Indian Industrial School visited, looking for boys. Al and his older brother volunteered to go, so he ended up back in Pennsylvania. Once again, Al had regular food, clothing, and shelter—but no Ojibwe community to nurture him and his cultural identity.

Like the school in Philadelphia, Carlisle also forced Native children to assimilate and adopt the culture and Christian religion of white people. Founded by US Army Colonel Richard Pratt, the school followed a strict military routine and schedule—which Al noticed right away. In the little free time he was allowed each afternoon, he enjoyed playing baseball with other boys.

Although he didn't see it at first, Carlisle's coach, Pop Warner, eventually recognized Al's tenacity, character, and competitive spirit when the young man pitched. Al then made the team and won his first game.

John's Journey to the Majors

After leaving school, Jack, now usually called John, worked for the Santa Fe railroad and played on the company's baseball team. When the railroad workers went on strike, John headed out on the road. He played baseball on semipro teams in Southern California and across the Southwest.

At a tournament in Albuquerque, New Mexico, a player on the opposing team became impressed with John's skills and size. He helped recruit John to play for Dartmouth College—in football and baseball. At five feet eleven and 194 pounds, John looked like a football player and yet had no interest in the game. He played baseball for one season there before the college found out he didn't have a high school diploma. When Dartmouth let John go, he moved on to the minor leagues, where he competed on four different teams.

PICKWICKS

SENATORS

BUTTE MINERS

ST. PAUL SAINTS

Charles's Quick Trip to the Pros

During Al's time at Carlisle, he developed his baseball skills. His keen eyesight and intelligence helped him craft pitches that confused and frustrated batters. After graduating in 1902, Al, now called Charles, signed with the Philadelphia Athletics and made his professional pitching debut the following year.

In his rookie season with the A's, nineteen-year-old Charles won seventeen games and pitched over two hundred innings—a rare feat in the twentieth century for a pitcher his age. Charles gave up only about three runs per game, and he seldom walked any batters—a sign of his impressive control. The powerhouse team was led by legendary manager Connie Mack (who always called Charles "Albert"). Mack coached many great pitchers during his fifty-year career, and he once said, "If everything depended on one game, I just used Albert."

John Heads to New York

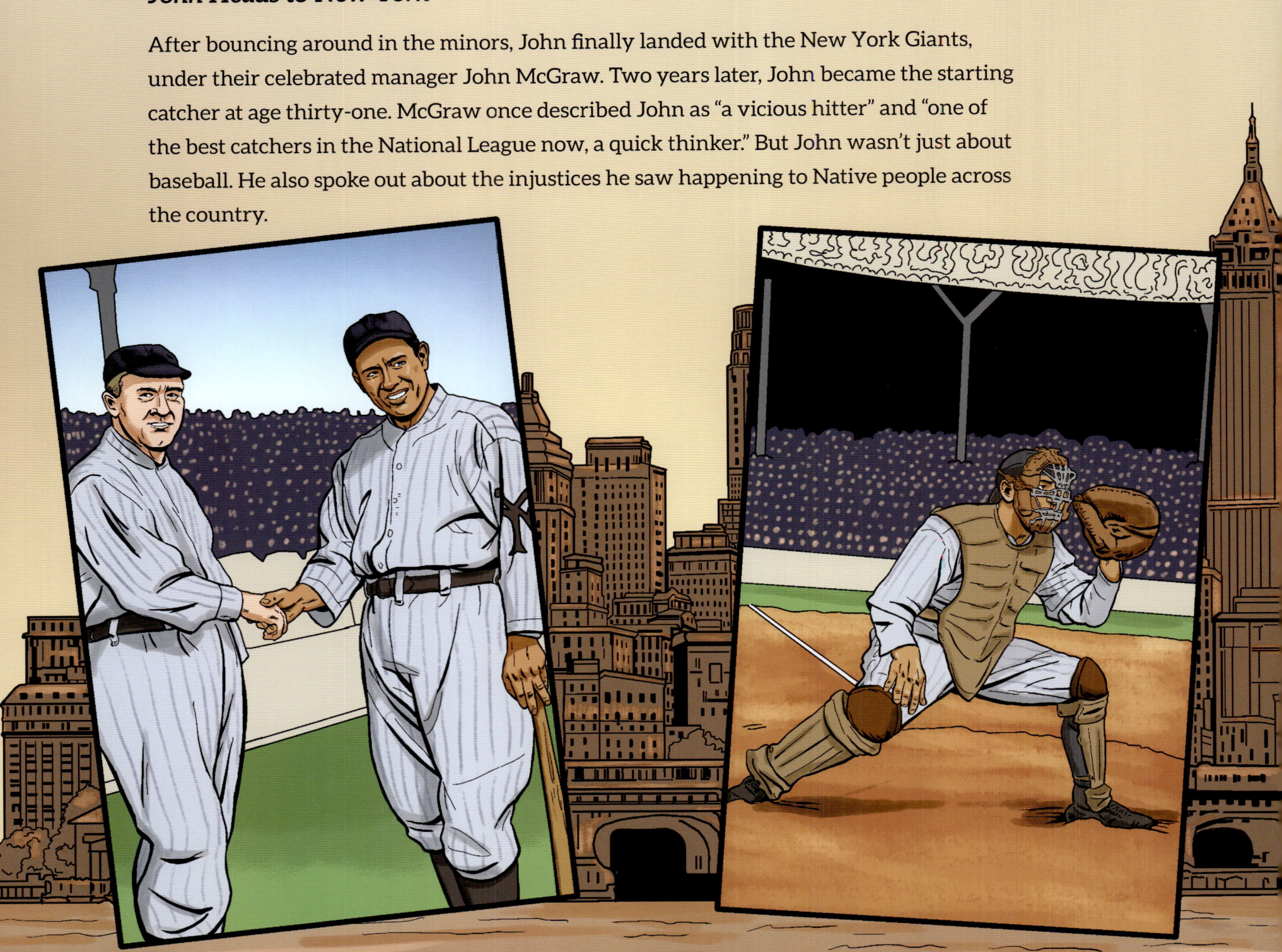

After bouncing around in the minors, John finally landed with the New York Giants, under their celebrated manager John McGraw. Two years later, John became the starting catcher at age thirty-one. McGraw once described John as "a vicious hitter" and "one of the best catchers in the National League now, a quick thinker." But John wasn't just about baseball. He also spoke out about the injustices he saw happening to Native people across the country.

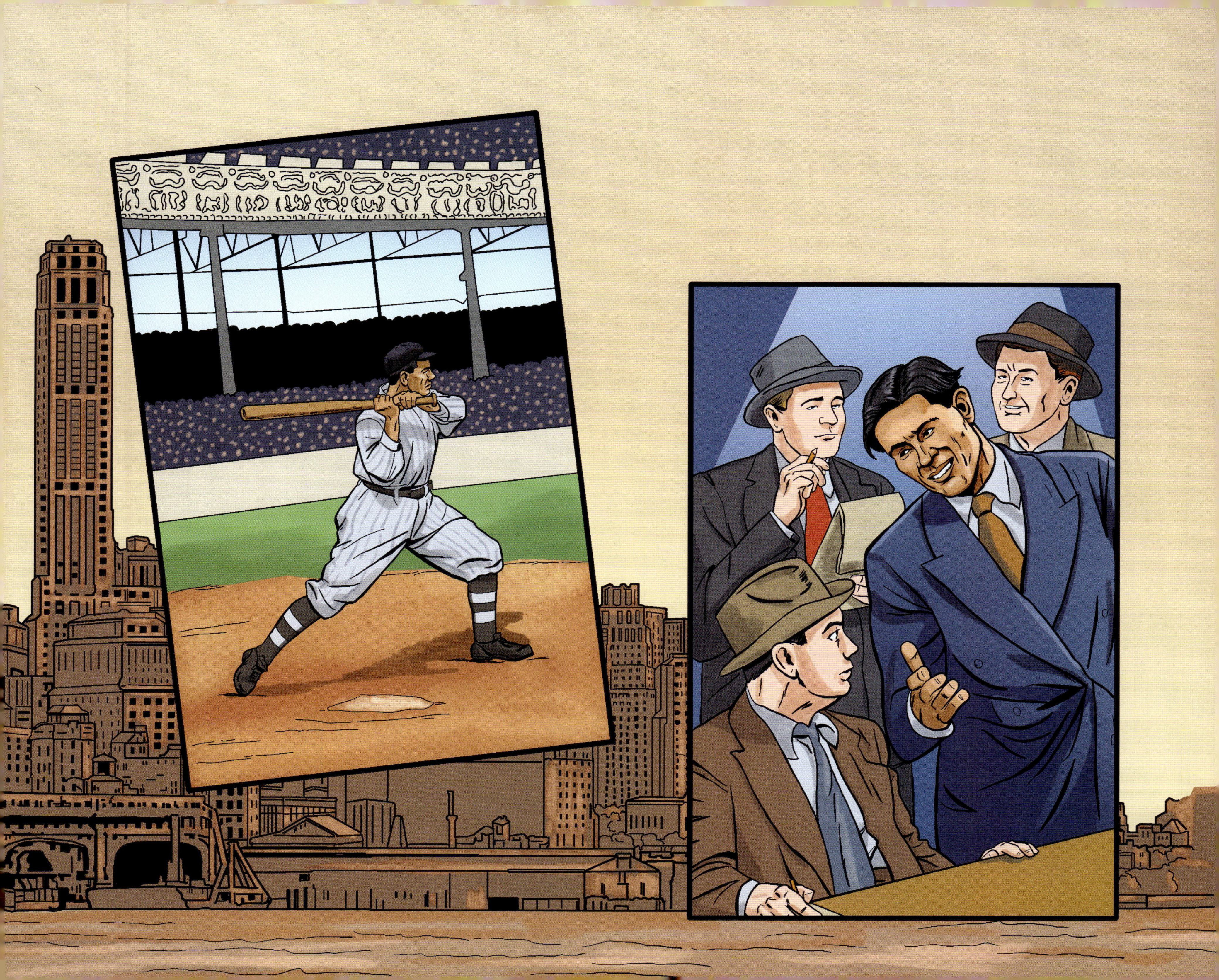

Enduring the Hate

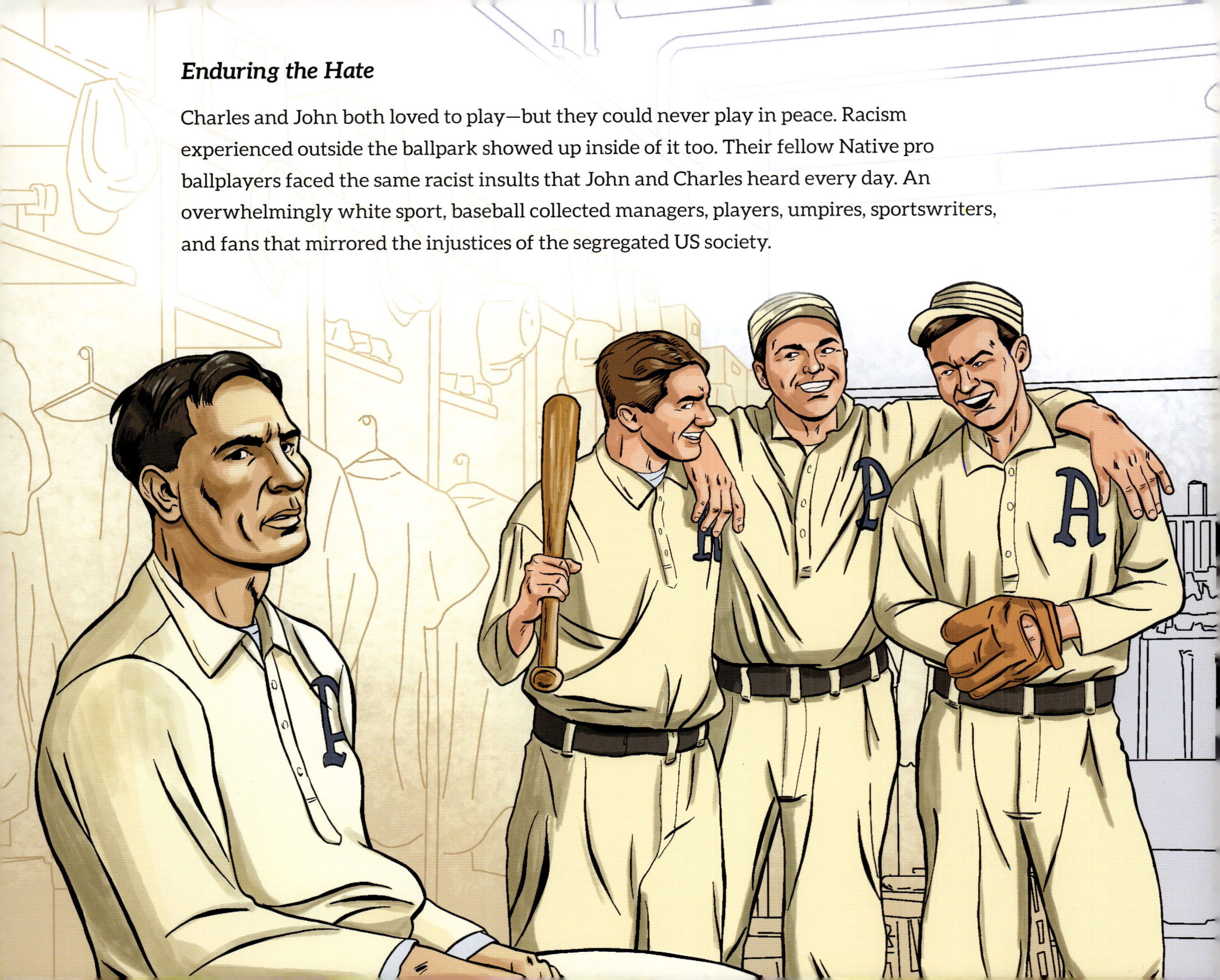

Charles and John both loved to play—but they could never play in peace. Racism experienced outside the ballpark showed up inside of it too. Their fellow Native pro ballplayers faced the same racist insults that John and Charles heard every day. An overwhelmingly white sport, baseball collected managers, players, umpires, sportswriters, and fans that mirrored the injustices of the segregated US society.

Regardless, Charles and John kept their game faces on. They each used their quick wit to deflect and defuse the insults and rude treatment—most of the time. Sometimes they shouted back. Still, both were determined to make a living playing the game they loved.

World Series Action: Friends Face Off

Just before the first game of the World Series in 1911, John poses on the field with Charles, whom he describes as "one of the nicest people you'd ever meet." The *New York Times* prints this line: "Maybe they wished they had tomahawks in their hands instead of a bat and a baseball." At the height of their careers, Charles and John can't escape the racism that infests even one of the country's leading newspapers.

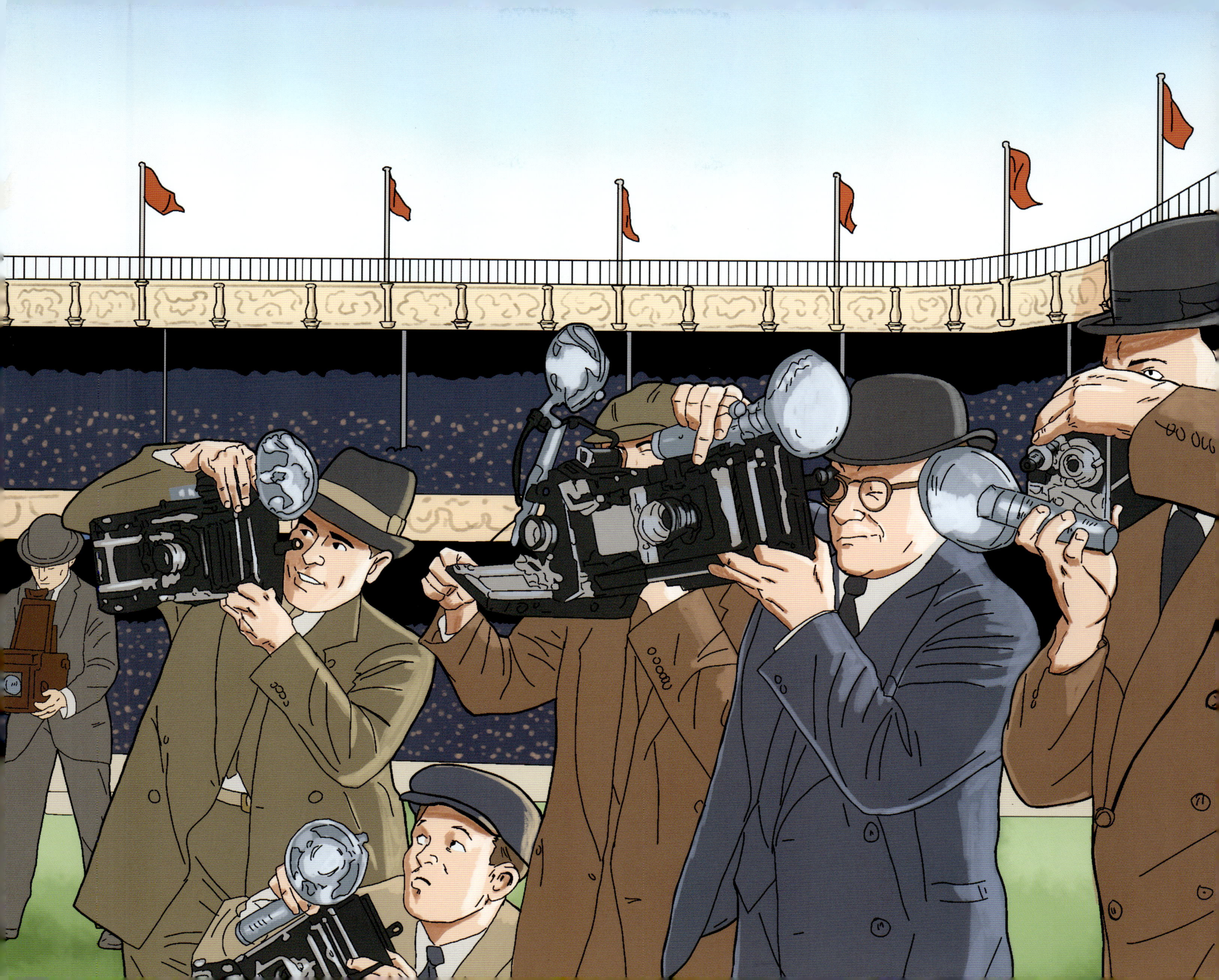

The New York Times.

OCTOBER 14, 1911.

World's Series.

Battling Back and Forth

Game One goes to the Giants, thanks to John's winning run.

But Charles's Athletics bounce back to take Game Two.

Game Three: close calls by the umpires, a dramatic home run, a high spikes-up slide by a Giants outfielder stealing third, and extra innings—including John's almost–home run at the top of the eleventh.

But the A's take the game and the Series lead.

And then: rain. For six days!

Wrapping It Up

When the Series resumes, Charles holds the Giants to just two runs in the first inning to win Game Four. The A's look ready to wrap the Series up.

But, in front of the home crowd, John's Giants eke out a win with a sacrifice fly in the tenth inning of Game Five.

Game Six: Charles pitches. The Giants struggle, getting only two runs off him.

His teammates back him up with their bats—scoring seven runs in the seventh inning alone. The A's win thirteen to two in front of their fans. The 1911 World Series champions!

Contenders Always

After the 1911 season, Charles and John kept playing, and they reached the World Series a combined nine times. But despite all their professional achievements, name-calling by those around them at the ballpark and racist cartoons and depictions in the newspapers persisted.

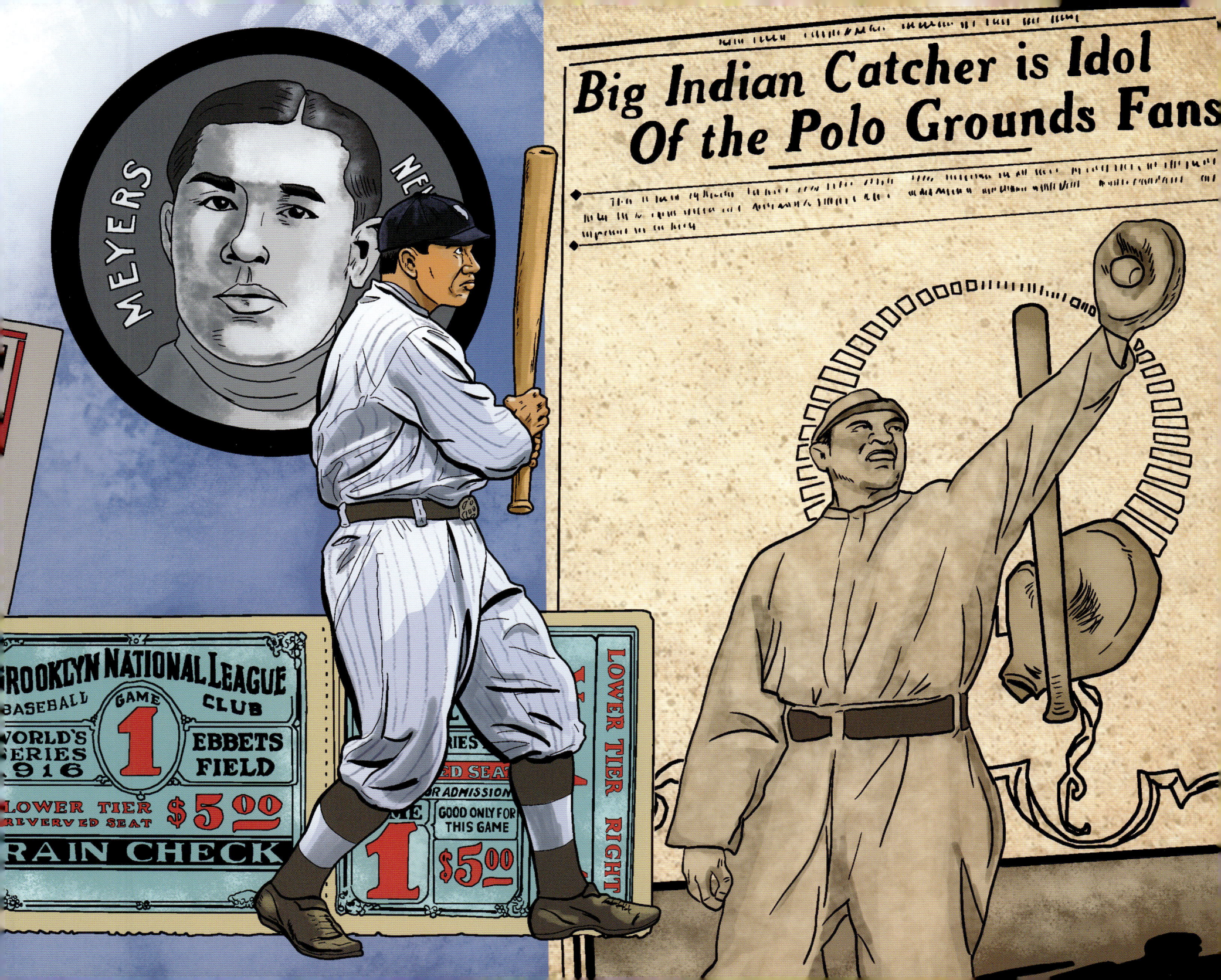

Big Indian Catcher is Idol Of the Polo Grounds Fans

More than one hundred years later, Native athletes today still face these same challenges. Tomahawk chops and derogatory chants and signs can be seen and heard at stadiums and ballparks across the country because of the permitted use of racist team mascots. From peewee to professional levels, no other athletes in the United States face the kind of sanctioned mocking and dishonor of their culture that Native players do.

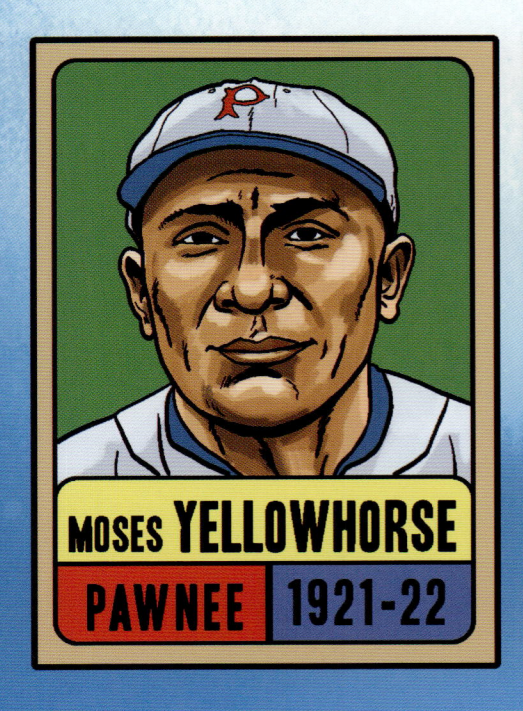

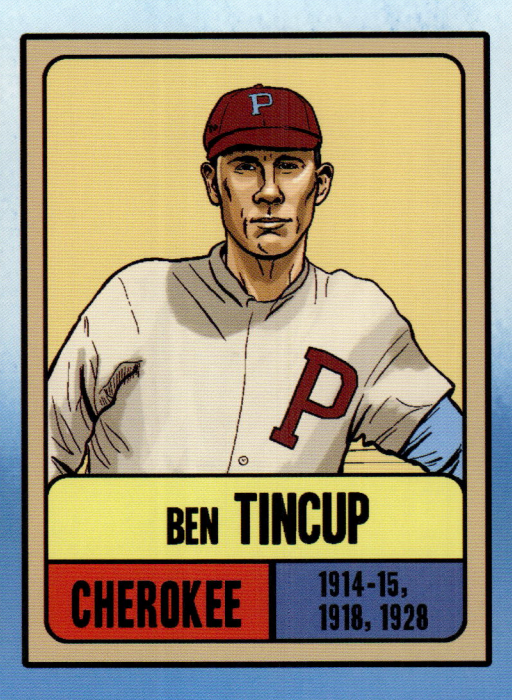

MOSES YELLOWHORSE — PAWNEE — 1921-22

JIM THORPE — SAC AND FOX — 1913-1915, 1917-1919

BEN TINCUP — CHEROKEE — 1914-15, 1918, 1928

ALLIE REYNOLDS — MUSCOGEE (CREEK) — 1942-1954

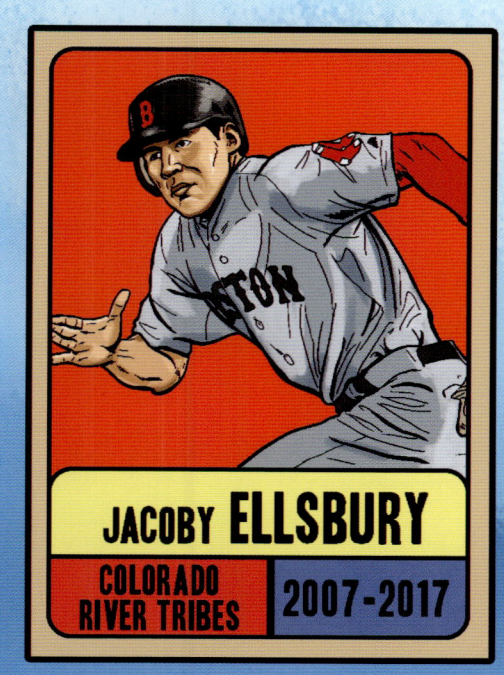

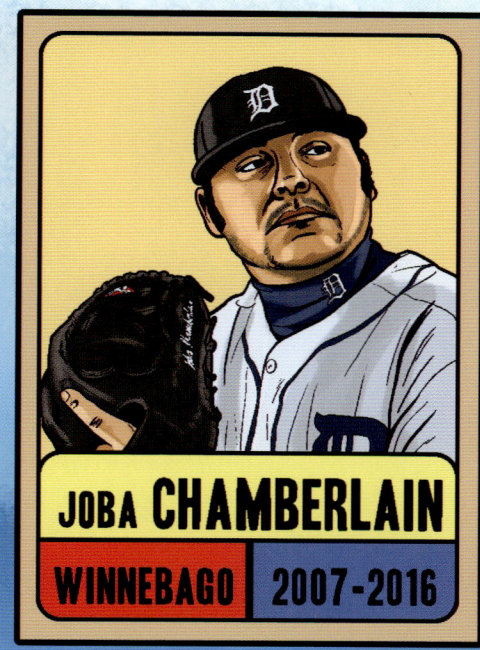

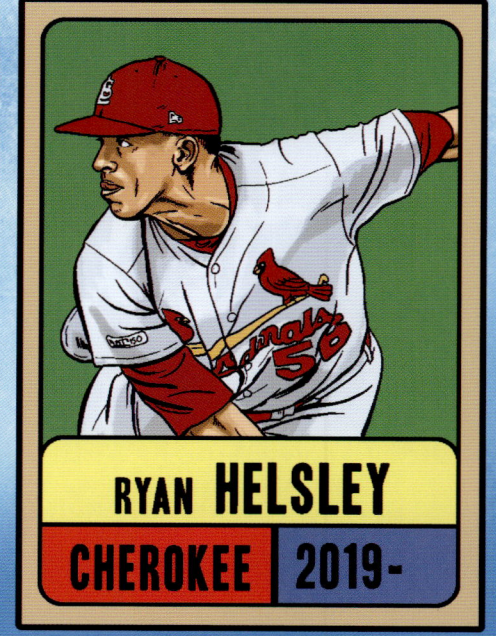

JACOBY **ELLSBURY**	JOBA **CHAMBERLAIN**	KYLE **LOHSE**	RYAN **HELSLEY**
COLORADO RIVER TRIBES	WINNEBAGO	WINTUN	CHEROKEE
2007–2017	2007–2016	2001–2018	2019–

Author's Note

Charles Bender and John Meyers faced off again in the 1913 World Series. While the Giants ended with a better regular-season record, they lost four games to one against the Athletics. Charles pitched the first and fourth games and won both. John injured his hand during warm-ups before the second game and sat out the rest of the Series, which hampered the Giants.

Over the course of his career, Charles pitched in five World Series with the A's and won three of them. In all, he played sixteen seasons in the big leagues, won 212 games, and posted a .625 winning percentage. He's credited with creating the slider, a pitch still used today in baseball, among an incredible list of other accomplishments. Charles stayed close to the game for the rest of his life, even managing minor-league teams in the east for a time. He was elected into the National Baseball Hall of Fame in 1953.

John caught in four championship series, but his teams never took home the trophy. He spent nine years in the majors and led the Giants in batting from 1911 to 1913 with a .332 average, the third highest in the National League at the time. He played and briefly managed in the minor leagues before leaving the game and returning to work on the Cahuilla reservation.

Time Line

1880 — John "Jack" Tortes Meyers is born in Riverside, California, in July to John Mayer and Felicité Tortes. He is a citizen of the Santa Rosa Band of Cahuilla Indians.

1884 — Charles "Al" Albert Bender is born in the Partridge Lake area of Crow Wing County, Minnesota, in May to Albertus Bliss Bender and Mary Razor. His maternal family is from the Mississippi Band of Ojibwe Indians.

1888 — The Bender family moves to the White Earth reservation in northwestern Minnesota, to tribal land allotted to their mother and her children. Citizens from several Ojibwe bands were relocated to this reservation.

1897 — Louis Sockalexis of the Penobscot Nation joins the Cleveland Spiders and becomes the first Native player in the National League, an independent professional baseball league in the United States at that time.

1903 — Two independent professional baseball leagues—the National League and the American League—combine to form Major League Baseball (MLB) and establish a "World Series," where the teams from both leagues play for an annual championship title.

1903 — Bender joins the Philadelphia Athletics as a starting pitcher. He is one of the tallest pitchers during that time at six feet two inches.

1904 — Bender marries Marie Clement of Detroit, Michigan.

1908 — At age 28, Meyers joins the New York Giants as a catcher late in the season. Jim Thorpe is his teammate from 1913 until the team waives Meyers's contract in 1915 and the Brooklyn Robins pick him up.

1909 — Meyers speaks up in defense of Chitto Harjo and other Muscogee Nation citizens who oppose the federal government's allotment of tribal lands.

1910 — Meyers marries Anna Brower of Maryland.

1917 — Meyers finishes his major-league career with the Boston Braves. Except for a cameo appearance in 1925 with the Chicago White Sox, Bender wraps up his MLB career with the Philadelphia Phillies, the National League crosstown rival of his former team, the A's.

1924 — All citizens of Native Nations receive US citizenship after President Calvin Coolidge signs the Indian Citizenship Act.

1947 — Jackie Robinson integrates MLB for African Americans on April 15.

1953 — Charles Bender is elected to the National Baseball Hall of Fame (NBHOF).

1954 — Bender dies in Philadelphia, Pennsylvania, on May 22 before the NBHOF induction ceremony in Cooperstown, New York, on August 9. His widow, Marie, accepts the plaque in his stead.

1971 — John Meyers dies on July 25 in San Bernardino, California.

1972 — Charles Bender and John Meyers are inducted into the American Indian Athletic Hall of Fame as part of the inaugural class.

2022 — Native baseball players still play in the major leagues, including four pitchers who are Cherokee Nation citizens: Dylan Bundy, Jon Gray, Ryan Helsley, and Adrian Houser. All pitch right-handed, like Bender.

Quotes

"Somebody . . . ball" Lampton

"Indian against Indian" Beach, p. 2

"Chief Bender" Ibid.

"Chief Meyers" Ibid.

"now . . . best Indian?" Ibid.

"redskins" Lampton

"If everything depended . . . used Albert" "Chief Bender Dies; A Famous Pitcher"

"vicious hitter" McGraw

"one of . . . thinker" Ibid.

"one of . . . ever meet" Ritter, p. 172

"Maybe they wished . . . baseball" Beach, p. 2

Sources

Baseball Reference. "Charles Bender". Accessed June 15, 2022. https://www.baseballreference.com/players/b/bendech01.shtml

"Jack Meyers." Accessed June 15, 2022. https://www.baseball-reference.com/players/m/meyerch01.shtml

Beach, Rex. "Giants Take First Game: Score 2 to 1." *New York Times*, October 15, 1911.

Kashatus, William C. *Money Pitcher: Chief Bender and the Tragedy of Indian Assimilation*. University Park: The Pennsylvania State University Press, 2006.

Koerper, Henry C. "The Catcher Was a Cahuilla: A Remembrance of John Tortes Meyers (1880–1971)." *Journal of California and Great Basin Anthropology* 24, no. 1 (30th Anniversary Issue (2002–2004)): 21–39.

Lampton, W. J. "Hits and Misses." *New York Times*, October 15, 1911.

McGraw, John. "Making a Pennant Winner." *Pearson's Magazine*, November 1912.

National Baseball Hall of Fame. "Charles Bender." Accessed June 15, 2022. https://baseballhall.org/hall-of-famers/Bender-Chief

"Chief Bender Dies; A Famous Pitcher." *New York Times*, May 23, 1954.

Nowlin, Bill. "Ralph Glaze." Society for American Baseball Research. Accessed June 15, 2022. https://sabr.org/bioproj/person/ralph-glaze/#

Philadelphia Athletics Historical Society. "Charles Albert "Chief" Bender: A Biographic Profile." Accessed June 15, 2022. https://www.philadelphiaathletics.org/charles-albert-chief-bender-a-biographic-profile/

Powers-Beck, Jeffrey. *The American Indian Integration of Baseball*. Lincoln: University of Nebraska Press, 2004.

Retrosheet. "The 1911 Post-Season Games." Accessed June 15, 2022. https://www.retrosheet.org/boxesetc/1911/YPS_1911.htm

Ritter, Lawrence S. *The Glory of Their Times: The Story of the Early Days of Baseball Told by The Men Who Played It*. New York: Macmillan, 1966.

Wiggins, Robert Peyton. *Chief Bender: A Baseball Biography*. Jefferson, North Carolina: McFarland & Company, 2010.

Young, William A. *John Tortes "Chief" Meyers: A Baseball Biography*. Jefferson, North Carolina: McFarland & Company, 2012.